n laughing eyes I see, the lo

dear on that pert and saucy

bow sash on your party dress,

weet, mommy's angel and

nk God in silent prayer for

k much dearer than all oth

of mine, can you ever kno

n laughing eyes I see, the lo

PRESENTED TO

FROM

DATE

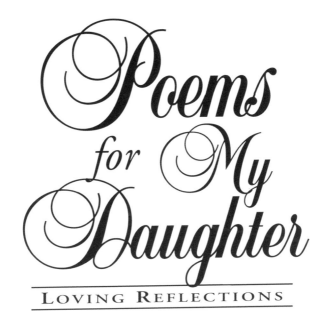

Poems for My Daughter

LOVING REFLECTIONS

WATERCOLORS BY
STACY VENTURI-PICKETT

IDEALS PUBLICATIONS
NASHVILLE, TENNESSEE

ISBN 0-8249-5846-2

Published by Ideals Publications, a division of Guideposts
535 Metroplex Drive, Suite 250, Nashville, Tennessee 37211
www.idealsbooks.com

Color separations by Precision Color Graphics, Franklin, Wisconsin
Printed and bound in the U.S.A. by Inland Press/Inland Book

Library of Congress Cataloging-in-Publication data on file

10 9 8 7 6 5 4 3 2 1

POEMS SELECTED BY JULIE K. HOGAN, PEGGY SCHAEFER
DESIGNED BY EVE DEGRIE

ACKNOWLEDGMENTS

BRADY, DANIEL J. "Her Sweet Smile." Used by permission of Daniel J. Brady. BURKET, GAIL BROOK. "To My Daughter." Used by permission of Anne E. Burket. DESMARAIS, ROGER. "Is This the Little Girl?" Used by permission of Roger Desmarais. EKLUND, GEORGE. "Dressing My Daughter" from *I Feel a Little Jumpy around You*. Selected by Naomi Shihab Nye and Paul B. Janeczko and published by Simon & Schuster Books for Young Readers, 1996. Reprinted by permission of George Eklund. HANDS, WILLIAM BRIGHTLY. "Polly" from *The World's Best Poetry, Vol. 1*. Copyright © 1981 by the Granger Book Company. HOCHMAN, SANDRA. "Thoughts about My Daughter before Sleep" from *A Mother's Book of Poems*, compiled by Christine M. Benton, Contemporary Books, 1994. Used by permission of Sandra Hochman. KLEMME, MINNIE L. "Little Girl with Daisies." Used by permission of Herbert L. Klemme. MICHAEL, PHYLLIS C. "Little Daughter of Mine." Used by permission of Phyllis C. Michael. OSTRIKER, ALICIA. "Hair" from *Green Age* by Alicia Suskin Ostriker. Copyright © 1989. Reprinted by permission of the University of Pittsburgh Press. PASTAN, LINDA. "Aubade" from *Tangled Vines: A Collection of Mother and Daughter Poems*, Harcourt Brace Jovanovich, 1992. Used by permission of the author. "Anna at Eighteen Months" and "To a Daughter Leaving Home" from *Carnival Evening*. Copyright © 1998 by Linda Pastan. Published by W.W. Norton and Company. SCHULTZ, GARNETT ANN. "To My Daughter." Used by permission of Garnett Ann Schultz. STRONG, PATIENCE. "Leaving Home" from *Friendship Book*. Copyright © 1962 by Patience Strong. Published by Frederick Muller, Ltd. Used by permission of Rupert Crew Limited. TURNER, ALBERTA. "Daughter, Daughter" from *Lid and Spoon* by Alberta Turner, Copyright © 1977. Reprinted by permission of University of Pittsburgh Press. Our sincere thanks to the following authors whom we were unable to locate: Gladys Cardiff for "Combing"; H. Charles Gallap for "Dear Daughter"; Magny Landstad Jensen for "What Shall I Wish For"; Edie Johnson for "Daughter"; The Estate of Inez Marrs for "Just As You Are Today"; Violet V. Moore for "Song in My Heart"; David C. Nichols for "At Midnight"; Pauline S. Roach for "Mommie's Hand"; Karl Shapiro for "Calling the Child"; Sharon F. Style for "Fly Softly, My Love"; Gail Todd for "To My Four-Year-Old Daughter"; David E. West for "Enchantress."

All possible care has been taken to fully acknowledge the ownership and use of every selection in this book. If any mistakes or omissions have occurred, they will be corrected in subsequent editions, provided notification is sent to the publisher.

CONTENTS

ALWAYS MY
LOVE

Two Lives

Two lives have changed,
Mine and yours.

My life comes from you.
Your life comes from above.

Together we live and grow
And teach each other love.
— AUTHOR UNKNOWN

To Annie

Annie, my firstborn, gentle child,
My tender, fragile flower,
Why twines thy image round my heart
With such mysterious power?

Is it because thy infant wail
The icy barrier moved,
That bound my soul's affections fast?
I knew 'twas mine I loved.

A mother's love no tongue can tell—
How boundless is that sea!
'Twas never mine; her spirit fled,
As she gave birth to me.

Annie, I gave to thee, my child,
The love my heart could yield;
God grant its influence o'er thee cast
From all life's ills a shield.
— MARY E. TUCKER

SONG IN MY HEART

Beneath a frame of dark brown hair,
The shadowed pools of jade
That are your eyes look out on life
And face it unafraid.

May all the joy you've given me,
Dear daughter, be yours too.
Oh, surely I am blessed to have
A treasure such as you.

You are the song within my heart,
Grown lovelier each year;
A muted melody of love
That I alone may hear.

— VIOLET V. MOORE

DAUGHTER OF MINE

Daughter of mine, can you ever know
How much you mean to me?
The precious joys that fill my heart
When your laughing eyes I see,
The loving caress and the tender cheek
I hold in fond embrace,
The precious dimple I love so dear
On that pert and saucy face.

Daughter of mine, with your tender heart,
Such a darling little girl,
A big bow sash on
your party dress,

A bow on a dancing curl,
Gentle and loving in every way,
So very dear and sweet,
Mommy's angel and Daddy's girl,
Our every dream complete.

Daughter of mine, this special day
I thank God in silent prayer
For the privilege of having you
Within my loving care.
I'm very proud of this special task
Much dearer than all other,
My heart is filled with joy untold
Each time you call me "Mother."
— GARNETT ANN SCHULTZ

THE MOTHER'S HOPE

Is there, when the winds are singing
    In the happy summertime,
When the raptured air is ringing
With Earth's music heavenward springing,
    Forest chirp, and village chime,
Is there, of the sounds that float
Unsighingly, a single note
Half so sweet and clear and wild
As the laughter of a child?

Listen! And be now delighted:
    Morn hath touched her golden string;
Earth and Sky their vows have plighted;
Life and Light are reunited
    Amid countless carolings;

Yet, delicious as they are,
There's a sound that's sweeter far,
One that makes the heart rejoice
More than all — the human voice!

Organ finer, deeper, clearer,
    Though it be a stranger's tone,
Than the winds or waters dearer,
More enchanting to the hearer,
    For it answereth to his own.
But of all its witching words,
Sweeter than the song of birds,
Those are sweetest, bubbling wild
Through the laughter of a child.

Harmonies from the time-touched towners,
  Haunted strains from rivulets,
Hum of bees among the flowers,
Rustling leaves, and silver showers,
  These, erelong, the ear forgets;
But in mind there is a sound
Ringing on the whole year round,
Heart-deep laughter that I heard
Ere my child could speak a word.

Ah! 'Twas heard by ear far purer,
  Fondlier formed to catch the strain,
Ear of one whose love is surer—
Hers, the mother, the endurer
  Of the deepest share of pain;

Hers the deepest bliss to treasure,
Memories of that cry of pleasure,
Hers to hoard, a lifetime after,
Echoes of that infant laughter.

'Tis a mother's large affection
   Hears with a mysterious sense,
Breathings that evade detection,
Whisper faint, and fine inflection,
   Thrill in her with power intense.
Childhood's honeyed words untaught
Hiveth she in loving thought,
Tones that never thence depart;
For she listens with her heart.

—LAMAN BLANCHARD

To My Daughter

I gather sunbeams in a golden skein
That I may weave a golden cloak for you.
With budding flowers I will embroider it
In glowing rose and morning glory blue.

For you I hoard the grace of swallow wings
And silver bravery of mountain streams.
I send you forth adorned in love and hope
And wearing my old diadem of dreams.

—GAIL BROOK BURKET

AUBADE

In the early morning
I shake my head
to clear away the static
of the dream,
the way my daughter
shakes the radio she holds
against her ear
as if it were a shell.

POEMS FOR MY DAUGHTER

On the table between us
the sun spreads
its slow stain;
fog lifts
from the coffee;
a heart drifts out of reach
on the surface
of the milk.
Now my daughter takes the day
into her hand
like fresh baked bread—
she offers me a piece.
— LINDA PASTAN

HER SWEET SMILE

I saw her smile
Just the other day
And that sweet smile
Took my breath away.

Suddenly her laughter
Filled the air;
I turned to look
And acquired a stare!

Two eyes of blue
Were shining bright
Throughout the day
And into the night.

And when she moves,
There's a certain grace
That complements
Her eyes and face.

Blond hair flows
And blue eyes dance;
Whenever I'm near her,
I'm lost in a trance,

Captivated by
Her precious smile
With moments to cherish
All the while.

I can't explain
Or understand;
She's an orchestral symphony
Played by a band.

This is the way
It always will be,
Living in my mind—
A glass menagerie.

All because
The other day
Her sweet smile
Took my breath away.
—DANIEL J. BRADY

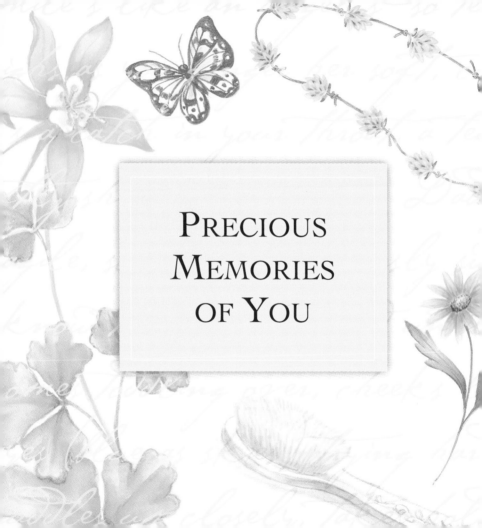

PRECIOUS
MEMORIES
OF YOU

NOT LONG AN INFANT

You were not long an infant.

The years when you leaped and bounded
Into childhood and inched into beyond
Have been astonishing.

Astonishing in their briefness,
Astonishing in their beauty.

Astonishing because all the years
wrapped around me,

Wrapped around you.
—AUTHOR UNKNOWN

ANNA AT EIGHTEEN MONTHS

Just as it did
for Eve,
language comes
tumbling in, word
by parroted word
as the world
is named again—
each beast and plant,
each bird.
For the floodgates
are open wide
and out of her dauntless
mouth spill

rough-hewn syllables
for elbow, eyes,
for chin.
And touched
by the wand
of the word, roused
from the alphabet's sleep,
new thoughts flutter awake
like butterflies utterly
changed,
like her damp flirtatious
lashes, beating
their tiny wings.
— LINDA PASTAN

MOMMIE'S HAND

Baby fingers cling to mine
As we climb the tall front stair;
 Small folk find the steps too steep
  Unless Mommie's hand is there.

 Just the slightest touch will do.
Baby voices cry with glee
As each hard-won height is gained,
"Here us coming, Mommie! See!"

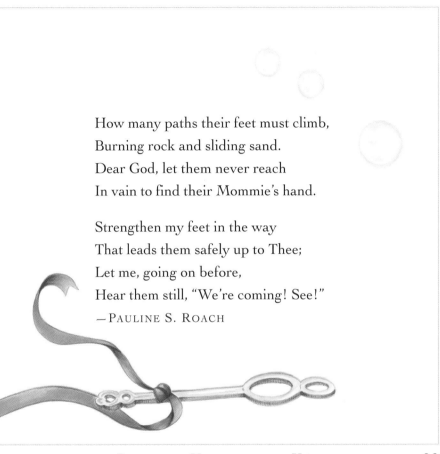

How many paths their feet must climb,
Burning rock and sliding sand.
Dear God, let them never reach
In vain to find their Mommie's hand.

Strengthen my feet in the way
That leads them safely up to Thee;
Let me, going on before,
Hear them still, "We're coming! See!"
—PAULINE S. ROACH

ENCHANTRESS

Her smile's like an angel's—so tender, so rare.
She sighs as you finger her soft, curly hair.
There's a catch in your throat, a tear in your eye
As softly she murmurs, "Hi, Daddy, Hi!"

So fragile, so tiny, so preciously sweet—
You know that she's played until "out on her feet."
She comes toddling over, cheeks like a rose,
Two eyes (blue as skies) trying hard not to close.

She cuddles up closely, takes hold of your hand;
She's just about set for the far-away land.
With a yawn and a chubby fist dug in each eye,
You help her along with a soft lullaby.

—DAVID E. WEST

AT MIDNIGHT

I tiptoe into your room.
There, bent over your crib,
I strain my eyes in an attempt to capture
A glimpse of your outline.

Gradually, by the illumination of the light in the hall,
I see you sleeping—your clown doll beside you,
Your arms folded behind your head,
Covered by a blanket which will soon be too small
For your lengthening limbs.

Listening to your measured breathing,
I think back two-and-one-half years.
Then, like most novice fathers,
My pulse quickened when, in your slumber,
I could not hear your infant breath.

Time and love have changed you
From a red-faced ball of precarious life
To a blond-headed vibrant human being,
A lady in miniature.

A lady!
How long will it be
'Till you leave your home for new places?
How many years of love-giving
Do your parents have left?

But that time is still far away.
'Tis wrong to live the future
Before the present is enjoyed.
Better to kiss you gently on the cheek
While you dream in your pink room.
—DAVID C. NICHOLS

POLLY

Brown eyes, straight nose;
Dirt pies, rumpled clothes;

Torn books, spoiled toys;
Arch looks, unlike a boy's;

Little rages, obvious arts;
(Three her age is), cakes,
    tarts;

Falling down off chairs;
Breaking crown down
    stairs;

Catching flies on the pane;
Deep sighs, cause not plain;

Bribing you with kisses
For a few farthing blisses;

Wide awake, as you hear,
"Mercy's sake, quiet, dear!"

New shoes, new frock;
Vague views of what's
    o'clock,

When it's time to go to bed,
And scorn sublime for what
   it said;

Folded hands, saying
   prayers,
Understands not, nor cares;

Thinks it odd, smiles away;
Yet may God hear her pray!
— WILLIAM BRIGHTLY HANDS

Dressing My Daughter

I have solved the riddle
of the three white buttons
but now you twist away from me
and all the muscle of my heart must hold
and help you understand.
Your mother has told me twice
the tiny pink bows
on these white anklets
must be turned
outward for the world
to see, to understand
you are a girl-child
and the pink bows
will help them see you
and help them remember
the words they are to say.

— George Eklund

CALLING THE CHILD

From the third floor I beckon to the child
Flying over the grass. As if by chance
My signal catches her and stops her dance
Under the lilac tree;
And I have flung my net at something wild
And brought it down in all its loveliness.
She lifts her eyes to mine reluctant,
Measuring in my look our twin distress.

Then from the garden she considers me
And, gathering joy, breaks from the closing net
And races off like one who would forget
That there are nets and snares.
But she returns and stands beneath the tree
With great solemnity, with legs apart,
And wags her head at last and makes a start
And starts her humorous marching up the stairs.

— KARL SHAPIRO

Is This the Little Girl?

I have a memory of you
As a little girl
Singing your heart out
On the stage of my heart,
In the halls of my mind,
Viewed from the orchestra pit
Of our family room.

I have a memory of you
As a young woman
During the last years of your childhood,
Before that stage of life when
Responsibility leads to accountability,
Yearning to be on with your life,
Displaying your courage and eagerness
To move on.

I have a memory of you
Looking back one last time,
About to turn away and walk into the
Future on your own,
Guided by whatever good
You have accepted from the past
And open to whatever good
Will be presented to you in the future.

— ROGER DESMARAIS

THE GIFT
YOU ARE

LITTLE GIRL WITH DAISIES

Little girl with an armful of daisies,
Out in the bright, sunny lea,
You have gathered the stars in the sky
And brought them along just for me.

And now you have offered your gift
And I have accepted your love.
Little girl with an armful of daisies,
What more can we share from above?

— MINNIE KLEMME

DEAR DAUGHTER

Little girl, little girl, my own little girl,
Grown up now and so far away,
Are you happy tonight? Are the stars shining bright?
Did the little ones have a good day?
Little girl, little girl, my own little girl,
As you walk down a strange new street,
Are you wearing a smile? Do you linger a while,
Making friends of the people you meet?

Little girl, little girl, my own little girl,
Is your task getting lighter somehow?
With a house full of love and a blue sky above,
Is your joy in the "here" and the "now"?
Little girl, little girl, my own little girl,
Give thanks for the treasures you hold.
Use the hours of each day as a potter with clay,
And the rest of your dreams will unfold.

—H. CHARLES GALLAP

DAUGHTER

I don't need to compete with her;
She's all that I would be,
And yet it is a knowing joy
That she is part of me.

Somewhere within her spirit gay
My quietness has rest,
And in the beauty of her dreams
My hopes are oft expressed.

This is the joy a daughter gives
Though she may never know it:
The fleeting bittersweet of life
As only youth can show it.

—EDIE JOHNSON

FLY SOFTLY, MY LOVE

First you smile
    and press her to your heart,
And the closeness is etched deeply forever.
But all too soon,
    with even that first step,
She begins on a path of her own.

Only she can follow it,
    can find her own true way.
So you laugh with her
    and love her gently away from you,

Encouraging her search,
   knowing that your heart is always open
   to her.

You give her the roots of home, of love,
Yet you show her the wings of peace.
   Fly softly, my love,
   My gentle, gentle dove.
—SHARI STYLE

HAIR

When I was the privileged woman, I wiped
The hair from your forehead
With its childish pucker, moist as a washcloth,

And when I was queen I brushed and braided it,
Pulled it away from your ears at the breakfast table,
Your ears as complicated as carnations—

Thus year followed year, like the eye-blink that human time
    Really is, until you decided
        I did it poorly, you could do it better, tighter

Yourself. So you brushed me off,
But my nose could reconstruct your ripe scalp-smell,
My palms the raw-silk feel of your springy strands.

When finally you sat in the hairdresser chair,
Child hair chopped off, as loose as brush
Around a clearing where someone is going to build,

I adored your face that rose, abrupt and pure,
A moon rising to survey the planet
By its own lucidity, while my hands

Were like lucky exiles who get away with everything.
Years after the revolution they still recall
The velvet ropes at the opera, that feel

Of unmistakable luxury.
—ALICIA OSTRIKER

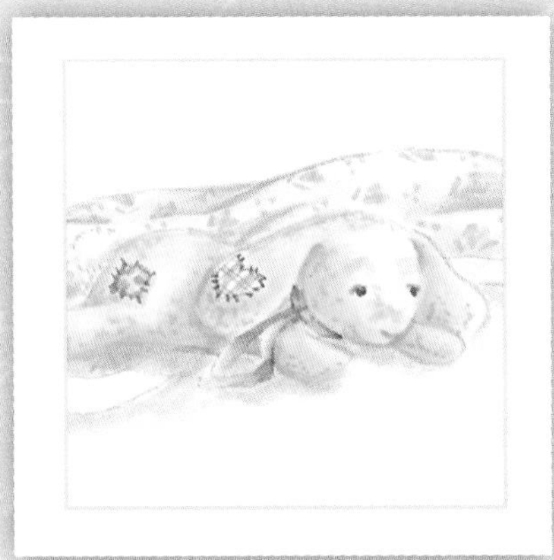

TO MY FOUR-YEAR-OLD DAUGHTER

I lost my temper twice today:
Once when you ordered me around like a maid
And once when you picked all the unripe plums from
    our tree.
You said I yelled so much it made you sleepy,
Popped in your thumb and drifted away.
Then, imagining you sad, I felt guilty.
You, my firstborn child, my beautiful girl.
Remember when your ear hurt and we rocked all night?
How many hours, awake, I stared in your face,
Seeing prongs that reach
Deep in your childhood, deep in mine.

— GAIL TODD

TO A DAUGHTER LEAVING HOME

When I taught you
at eight to ride
a bicycle, loping along
beside you
as you wobbled away
on two round wheels,
my own mouth rounding
in surprise when you pulled
ahead down the curved
path of the park,

I kept waiting
for the thud
of your crash as I
sprinted to catch up,
while you grew
smaller, more breakable
with distance,
pumping, pumping
for your life, screaming
with laughter,
the hair flapping
behind you like a
handkerchief waving
goodbye.
—LINDA PASTAN

COMBING

Bending, I bow my head
And lay my hand upon
Her hair, combing, and think
How women do this for
Each other. My daughter's hair
Curls against the comb,
Wet and fragrant—orange
Parings. Her face, downcast,
Is quiet for one so young.

I take her place. Beneath
My mother's hands I feel
The braids drawn up tight
As a piano wire and
   singing,
Vinegar-rinsed. Sitting
Before the oven I hear
The orange coils tick
The early hour before
   school.
She combed her grand-
   mother
Mathilda's hair using
A comb made out of bone.

Mathilda rocked her oak
   wood
Chair, her face downcast,
Intent on tearing rags
In strips to braid a cotton
Rug from bits of orange
and brown. A simple act,

Preparing hair. Something
Women do for each other,
Plaiting the generations.
— GLADYS CARDIFF

TALISMAN

All heaven in my arm,
The child for a charm
'Gainst fear and 'gainst sorrow,
Today and tomorrow.
The child for a charm
Betwixt me and harm.

O mouth, full of kisses!
Small body of blisses!
Your hand on my neck
And your cheek to my cheek.
What shall hurt me or harm
With all heaven in my arm?
— KATHARINE TYNAN HINKSON

Thoughts about My Daughter before Sleep

Ariel, one true
Miracle of my life, my golden
Sparrow, burning in your crib
As the rain falls over the meadow
And the squirrel corn,
While the fragrant hyacinth
    Sleeps in its bed in the rich
    Mud of the north, while foamflowers
    Climb through small arches of rain, and the sun
Brings lilies and dark blue berries
In cluster, leaf on leaf again,
I wonder how I came to give you life.

Here, where the twisted stalks
Of deer grass zigzag
Branches from the tree, where
Honeysuckles trumpet, "All joy
Is in the dark vessels of the skin!"
And thorn apples open their leaves,
I marvel to have made you perfect
As a small plant, you, filled
Up with sunlight and
Fragrant as ferns.

And before snow
Covers ivy and bluet
Shall I teach you this old
Summer's lesson
About seeds? About miracles
Of growth? Here are the bursting zinnias,
Asters, prongs
Of phlox — shall I wake you?
Take you out of sleep
And roll you in the apple fields?

And through you
I am born as I lie down
In the seedbox of my own beginnings,
Opening the wild part of me,
Once lost once lost
As I was breathing
In the vines of childhood.
—SANDRA HOCHMAN

DAUGHTER, DAUGHTER

When you peel an egg, leave the skin.
If you jump rope, drop the loop.
A pound of feathers equals a pound of axes.

Blackbirds don't make good pies.
Fill a fruit pie twice as full.
Tin coughs, glass gargles, sand swallows.

Steal only what you can wear.
Two nickels don't ring like a dime.
Saints come in pints, quarts, gallons.

Step on a crack, break your mother's back;
Skip one, break your own.

Seeds are round.
Shells listen.

—ALBERTA TURNER

SWEET HOPES
AND DREAMS

WHAT SHALL I WISH FOR?

What shall I wish for you, daughter mine,
Beauty, fortune, or raiment fine?
Friendship, power, or fickle fame,
Bold adventure to light a flame?
Heart that is tender, trusting and true,
Eager and gallant the soul in you;
Mind untarnished and spirit strong,
Serving life with a will and a song—
All of these purposes, noble, fine,
Do I wish for you, daughter mine!

— MAGNY LANDSTAD JENSEN

The Years Ahead

I cannot tell you what the years may hold,
Nor what of gain or loss may come to you,
I but repeat what has been often told,
A few brief maxims, old, but ever true.

'Tis not the prize but how the game was played;
'Twixt right and wrong all men at times must choose.
Keep this in mind before the choice is made:
It isn't triumph if your fame you lose.

Work hard, fight hard, and do the best you can;
Deserve the victory or refuse the prize.
'Tis better far to be the beaten man
Than take the glory and yourself despise.

This frenzied world, so clamorous for gain,
This troubled world, where man his years must spend
Still honors all who steadfastly remain
Gracious and just and faithful to the end.

—AUTHOR UNKNOWN

Just as You Are Today

I wish I could return to you
The joy you've given me.
I wish the moon was mine to give
But that can never be.

I wish I could erase your tears
Each night and every day.
I wish that you could always smile
And be forever gay.

I wish that I could give you faith,
For it is heaven's key,
And with God as your lifelong friend,
You'd conquer adversity.

I wish that I could give you love
Enough for all mankind,

So you could love as I love you,
With heart and soul and mind.

I wish that I could give you hope
The days you're sad and blue,
Then prove to you I truly care
And that your friends care too.

I wish these things were mine to give,
Yet that would not be fair,
For your life wouldn't be complete
Without burdens to bear.

But if one wish were granted me,
I'd wish you'd always stay
As beautiful, as gay and bright,
Just as you are today.

—INEZ MARRS

THE MOTHER'S WISH

May cloudless beams of grace and truth
Adorn my daughter's op'ning youth!
Long, happy in her native home,
Among its fragrant groves to roam,
May choicest blessings her attend,
    Blest in her parents, sisters, friends!
        May no rude wish assail her breast
        To love this world, by all confest
    As only giv'n us to prepare
    For one eternal, bright and fair.

This world shall then no force retain,
Its siren voice shall charm in vain;
Religion's aid true peace will bring,
Her voice with joy shall praises sing
To Him whose streams of mercy flow
To cheer the heart o'ercharged with woe;
And whilst retirement's sweets we prove,
Forever praise redeeming love.

—ANN AND JANE TAYLOR

LITTLE DAUGHTER OF MINE

Little daughter of mine, I'd give you the world
If it were mine to give;
I'd give you its sunbeams, its roses, its dew
To keep as long as you live.

But since it's not mine to give you these things,
There's a wish I'd wish instead:
May you have for your own, some, bright golden day,
A sweet little curly head—

A daughter as fine as you've always been,
A sweet little girl of your own,
Then you'll be as happy as I am today;
You'll be a queen on her throne.
—PHYLLIS C. MICHAEL

WISHES FOR MY DAUGHTER

To have faith in yourself,
To respect yourself and others,
To give freely and expect nothing in return,
To laugh whenever you can,
To know no fear.

To share your joy freely,
To love unabashedly,
To speak earnestly,
To listen honestly.

To find a dream and follow it,
To always do the best you can,
To make your laurels but not to rest on them.

To live in peace,
To be securely happy,

To thank God for your life.
—AUTHOR UNKNOWN

To My Daughter Mary on Her Eighteenth Birthday

So! Leap the limit now that parts
The woman from the child;
   Enter life's great career at last —
    No more with toys beguiled.

   Earth spreads its pageant at thy feet;
The bright world opens wide.
Go, be a woman, glad assume
The toils which thee abide!

   Or joy, or woe — no tongue can tell
   What fate thy lot may be,
  But meet it bravely, strong in faith,
  God rules thy destiny.

Like breezes o'er the bending grain,
Like sunlight on the wave,
Earth's rapid joys and trials pass;
Jehovah lives to save.

Go, be a woman; round thy path
Make love and gladness spring;
Reap in all fields; from every task
Some sheaves of goodness bring.

So shall life's current cheerful flow,
So bright shall be thy days;
No flattering words shall make thy fame;
Thy works shall be thy praise.

— Reverend Samuel Francis Smith

THE GIFT

I want to give you something, my child,
for we are drifting in the
stream of the world.
Our lives will be carried apart
and our love forgotten.
But I am not so foolish
as to hope
that I could buy your heart
with gifts.
Young is your life,
your path long,
and you drink the love
we bring you
at one draught and turn
and run away from us.

You have your play and your playmates.
What harm is there if you have not time
or thought for us.

We, indeed, have leisure enough
in old age to count
the days that are past,
to cherish in our hearts
what our hands have lost forever.

The river runs swift with a song,
breaking through
all barriers.

But the mountain stays and remembers
and follows her with his love.

—RABINDRANATH TAGORE

Leaving Home

The time has come to spread your wings
and leave the family nest—
your own way in the world to make.
Oh may that way be blessed
with happiness and all success.
This is our wish for you:
that you'll fulfill the highest hopes and reach the goal in view.

Write as often as you can and tell us how you fare.
There'll be problems and temptations all around you there
but never let your standards fall.
Be good and straight and true,
remembering the faith and trust that has been placed in you.

—Patience Strong

A Farewell

My fairest child, I have no song to give you;
    No lark could pipe to skies so dull and gray;
Yet, ere we part, one lesson I can leave you
    For every day:

Be good, sweet maid, and let who will be clever;
    Do noble things, not dream them, all day long:
And so make life, death, and that vast forever
    One grand, sweet song.
— CHARLES KINGSLEY

TITLE INDEX

Author Index

POEMS FOR MY DAUGHTER

First Line Index

First Line Index